Stevenson
Language
Skills
Program

BEGINNING I
WORKBOOK
BOOK B

By NANCY STEVENSON
AND
JANICE L. SEMPLE

Illustrated By Janice L. Semple

PUBLISHER
Stevenson Learning Skills, Inc.
8 Commonwealth Avenue
Attleboro Falls, MA 02763

Printed in the United States of America

ISBN 0-941112-07-1

7890TS987654

To The Teacher

The pages of this workbook are correlated to the lessons in the Stevenson Beginning I Teacher-Student Manual. Each page is designed to reinforce the learning of a specific integral whether it be a single letter, a letter pattern, a word or a concept. The student will move through these work sheets in stages. For example, the pages correlated to Lessons 1-9 will require the student to use a considerable amount of conscious, focused attention in order to complete the activity. By Lesson 15 the decoding and encoding of letters and letter patterns begin to become automatic for many of the students. At this point the student is introduced to new information that requires a higher degree of focused attention. As the student is acquiring new skill, he processes words by a combination of automatic response and focused attention. Throughout the workbook the student's attentional system is exercised regularly and thoroughly. When new information is introduced, the activity is relatively simple to perform. Then, as the student grows more adept at processing the integrals, the activities become more complex. This pattern of moving from the simple to the complex and back to the simple is maintained throughout the book in order to relieve some of the student's burdens and give him time to absorb procedual rituals.

Although the obvious purpose of this workbook is teaching the student how to decode and encode the integrals, the book is designed to develop other areas of proficiency as well. These other skills are more general in nature and are required in many areas of the student's educational performance. While many students acquire competence easily, almost as a by-product of their education, others who are neurologically immature or perceptually handicapped must work hard initially and practice regularly in order to become competent. The list below identifies some of these important skills. The pages of the workbook are designed to exercise these abilities. The teacher should be able to progress more effectively by keeping them in mind when working with the student. While the pupil is doing the workbook activities, he should be taught to:

Isolate- After examining the whole configuration, select the pertinent letter or letter pattern needed to accomplish the task. Be able to suppress temporarily the peripheral material.

Discriminate - Perceive differences in the shapes, sizes or patterns of letters.

Associate - Connect a concrete clue with an abstraction. For example, relating the shape and sound of a snake with the letter s.

Experience - Assume the qualities and motives of the concrete item associated with the letter or letters. For example, making the sound of a snake when personifying the snake letter s.

Identify - Equate the abstraction with the quality of the concrete clue. In other words, establish the ability to cross over from symbol to sound and from sound to symbol.

Express in writing - Represent graphically the letter or letters on paper and develop a sense of direction in order to reproduce a specific symbol regularly and accurately.

COMMENTS

1. The instructor should carefully teach the lesson from the Stevenson Teacher–Student Manual before the student is assigned the workbook pages for that lesson.

2. The teacher must give careful directions that the student can follow each time he starts a new page. Not until the end of the Basic Level of the Stevenson Program does the individual begin to read and interpret the directives independently.

3. Only those pages that require focused attention in all or part of the activity have been included in the workbooks. The sequence of operations that the child is to develop was chosen after years of testing on a variety of types of students.

4. The teacher may find that at least one third of the class has difficulty in many areas. These people often struggle when copying material. Keep in mind the number and complexity of skills required in this task. The best approach when expecting the student to copy a letter shape five times would be to have the letter repeated five times on the line above. Shifting the eyes up and down does not distort the focus as much as having to shift the eyes from side to side. The Stevenson Program will eventually have exercise books that allow for this adjustment.

5. The printing in the puzzles and in other places was done by hand rather than by typeface so that the student begins to be exposed to variations in handwriting. Students have to learn that letters may appear in different styles.

6. Do not criticize poor coloring results. Staying within the lines is an almost impossible neurological task for some. If a paper is a complete disaster you could first compliment the effort and then gently suggest to the student that he will improve because you know he is working hard. On the coloring pages there are lined spaces beside the color names. The teacher should fill in the color in this space with crayon because many students cannot sight read these words.

7. After the student has learned to print his name, he should always fill in that space on the page. The child's name can be written on a card and taped to his desk for him to copy. By mid-year, if he is ready, the date should be included.

8. The student should be told that the printing lines of the workbook pages represent houses. The upper solid line is the roof of the house and the lower solid line is the floor. The dotted line represents the ceiling. (Some children may need to be shown what a two story house looks like.) This concrete spatial orientation helps the student when he is beginning to print. He is told that letters such as g and j which reach below the floor go down to the cellar. With the concrete clue in mind it is easier for the student to choose the correct placement for the letter.

9. The older student can skip the coloring pages. We, however, have been amazed to find that even the high school student has wanted to do the coloring. We need to remember that learning disabled students often could not color well in the early grades and later get satisfaction out of seeing a job well done.

Book I Bg.   Lesson 29 Layer Cake <u>a</u>   Integral 49

Teacher: Student underlines the correct word and copies it in the space in
the sentence. Another day the student can answer the questions with <u>yes</u> or
<u>no</u>.

1. Could Kay go into a_____? _____
             cake   cave   cane

2. Does a cave have a _____? _____
             page   gate   fate

3. Can Jake wait at the_____? _____
             fate   page   gate

4. Does the seal have a_____? _____
             male   name   lane

5. Could Jake_____ a cake for Jane?_____
       bale   base   bake

6. Can a goat_____ to Jane? _____
       wake   wave   cave

Book I Bg.   Lesson 29 Layer Cake <u>a</u>   Integral 49

Teacher: Divide your class into small groups. Explain the directions for this
activity to each group separately. Take the students through the first column
to see if they understand the directions you give. Tell your pupils to imagine
they have a giant sized case that they can put things into. It is so big they
could even put a boat or a house in this case. It is also waterproof. Now they
are to read the words in the list #1 and put <u>x</u>'s beside the things that you can
put in the giant sized case. (Ex. cake, game etc.) After they have put <u>x</u>'s by
the words, they are then to make pictures of the words and copy the correct word
underneath each of the pictures. This is a complex directive so remember to take
those that need extra help very slowly through the procedure. The page can be
used six separate times by using the various columns. (This exercise is the beginning of what will eventually lead to work with nouns.)

1

1. cake
2. lame
3. late
4. game
5. mean
6. bake

2

1. meat
2. Jane
3. rake
4. safe
5. tame
6. save

3

1. came
2. gate
3. rave
4. cane
5. Jake
6. lame

4

1. lake
2. name
3. fate
4. Dave
5. cape
6. dare

5

1. sail
2. wave
3. fate
4. Jake
5. pail
6. tail

6

1. lake
2. maid
3. fame
4. dame
5. mail
6. nail

Book I Bg.   Lesson 29 Layer Cake <u>a</u>   Integral 49

Teacher: Explain to the student that p+j in the future will represent <u>peanut</u> butter and <u>jelly</u> words (emphasize the <u>p</u> and the <u>j</u> sounds in the words).   Also l-c will represent <u>layer cake</u> words. Student colors as follows:

p+j____green   open sand.____red

l-c____blue   ai=ay____yellow

Book I Bg.   Lesson 29 Layer Cake <u>a</u>   Integral 49

Teacher: Student answers the questions by circling <u>yes</u> or <u>no</u>. The circle
should start at the dot and continue from right to left. After answering
the questions, the student is to make a picture of the statement below.

1. Could Jake make a game?   no˙ yes˙

2. Can Jane sail in a cave?   no˙ yes˙

3. Can Jean wave to Jane?   no˙ yes˙

4. Would Jake care to eat a rake?   no˙ yes˙

5. Would Jane hate a mean goat?   no˙ yes˙

6. Could Dean be a name?   no˙ yes˙

Make Jake rake the road.

Book I Bg.   Lesson 30 Soft and Hard <u>c</u>   Integrals 3, 50

Teacher: Reteach the lesson from the manual by explaining that if <u>c</u> has curled
up <u>e</u> friend beside him the <u>c</u> turns himself into a snake and makes the hissing
snake sound for his letter <u>c</u>. If the <u>c</u> has a letter right next to him (right
side) that does not look like a snake, he keeps his <u>k</u> sound. Student looks at
the list of words and writes them in the correct columns.

coat

lace

cape

cake

face

cave

race

came

1. The _____ is in the case.
   coat face race

2. The _____ is on the coat.
   race lace care

3. The _____ on the deer is neat.
   lace race face

4. Dave can go in the _____.
                 lace cane cave

5. Jane _____ to the game.
   face came care

6. Jake made a _____ cape.
       race face lace

Book I Bg.   Lesson 30 Soft <u>c</u>   Integral 50

Teacher: The student makes lines to match the words in the columns. Then
he finds and circles those same words in the puzzle - across and up to down
only. He may cross off a line beside the word in the column after he finds
it in the puzzle. Some students find this crossing off process difficult.
If the task is too frustrating, it can be ignored. The student writes the
words in the spaces below. He can decorate the page afterwards.

race   lace |||||||

face   race ||||||

lace   face |||||

l	a	c	e	f	a	c	e	r
a	l	r	l	a	c	e	r	a
c	f	r	a	c	e	f	a	c
e	f	a	c	e	r	a	c	e
r	a	c	e	l	a	c	e	a
l	r	a	l	a	c	e	e	c

_____ | _____ | _____

Book I Bg.   Lesson 31   Layer Cake <u>a</u>   Layer Cake <u>i</u>   Integrals 49, 51

Teacher: See directions in Lesson 10. Student reads the words in the first
list and puts <u>x</u>'s beside six layer cake <u>i</u> words. He prints these on the
illustrated layer cake page. At another time, he finds the layer cake <u>a</u>
words in the second list and follows the same procedure.

Layer Cake <u>i</u>

cane	lime	cape
mile	lame	wipe
lake	hike	bite
side	bake	rate
rake	wave	name

Layer Cake <u>a</u>

race	face	rake
rice	nice	game
date	kite	life
dime	dare	mine
hike	bite	pine

Book I Bg.   Layer Cake Words   Integrals 49, 51, 54, 57

Teacher: Student uses this page with layer cake words. With the arrow pointed
away from his stomach, he puts the letters in the correct spaces of the cake.
He then prints the word twice in the spaces below the picture.

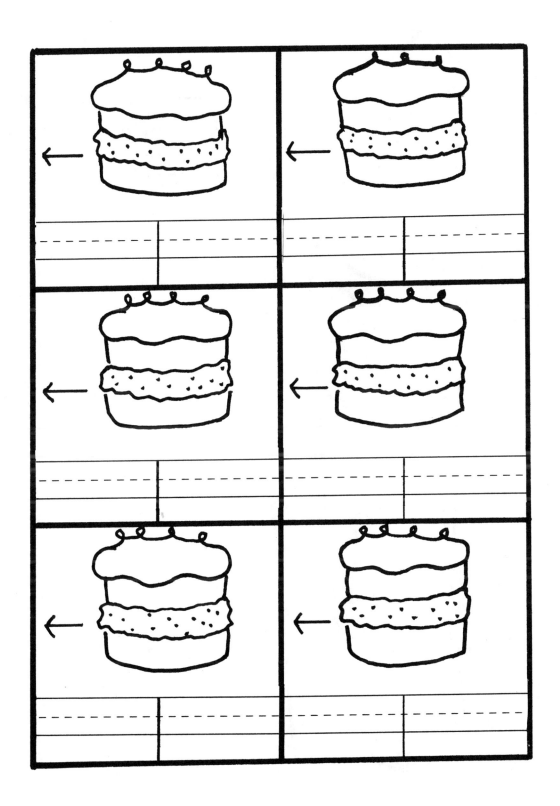

Book I Bg.   Lesson 31 Layer Cake <u>i</u>   Integral 51

Teacher: Be sure to fill in the color with a crayon in the space beside
the word. The student does not know these sight words. Student colors
the picture as follows:

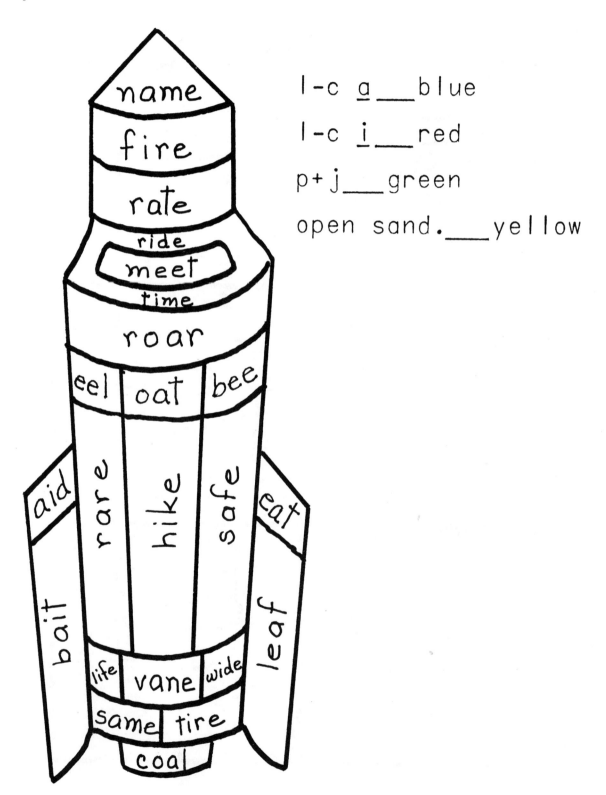

l-c <u>a</u> ___ blue

l-c <u>i</u> ___ red

p+j ___ green

open sand. ___ yellow

Book I Bg.   Lesson 31 Layer Cake <u>a</u> and <u>i</u>   Integrals 49, 51

Teacher: Student circles the words and may cross off a line beside the word in the column after he finds it in the puzzle. If the crossing off task is too frustrating, it can be ignored.

dice | | | | nice | | | |
face | | | pace | |
lace | | | race | | |
lice | | | | rare |
mice | | | | | rice | | | |

face

d	l	r	a	c	e	h	m	n	h	r
m	i	c	e	b	d	n	i	c	e	a
d	c	c	b	p	l	i	c	e	l	c
i	e	n	e	r	a	r	e	d	f	e
c	g	b	i	i	c	c	i	b	a	r
e	d	f	a	c	e	r	e	c	c	i
n	m	i	c	e	e	l	a	c	e	c
i	l	i	c	e	f	l	i	c	e	e
c	d	i	c	e	l	a	c	e	e	d
e	n	i	c	e	m	i	c	e	h	n
r	i	c	e	i	p	a	c	e	r	b

Book I Bg.   Lesson 31 Layer Cake <u>i</u>   Integral 51

Teacher: Each day help the student fold a paper into fours. He is to read a section and make the pictures of what he reads. (See directions in Lesson 9.)

1. Make Dave ride a bike. 2. Make Jane eat a lime. 3. Make a pipe. 4. Make five mice.

1. Make Dean dive in the lake. 2. Make a dime. 3. Make a bee hive. 4. Make a nice cake.

1. Make a pile of pea<u>s</u>. 2. Make a wide line. 3. Make a kite. 4. Make a tire.

1. Make an eel. 2. Make Jane eat rice. 3. Make Jean hike on the road. 4. Make mice hide near a pail.

Book I Bg.   Lesson 31 Buzzing <u>s</u>   Integral 52

Teacher: Student circles the words and may cross off a line beside the
word in the column after he finds it in the puzzle. If the crossing off
task is too frustrating, it can be ignored.

fuse	I I I I I
hose	I I I I
nose	I I I I
pose	I I I
rise	I I I I
rose	I I I I I
wise	I I I I I

```
r n f n h n o s e c d
m o u p o s e h o s e
w i s e s s h o s e b
r w e e e c e r o s e
o i f u s e p o s e p
s s s r i s e s d r o
e e c e f u s e b i s
w h o s e w s f g s e
r i s e c o i u u e h
n o s e p r o s e s n
w i s e n o s e e r e
```

Book I Bg.   Lesson 31 Buzzing <u>s</u>   Integral 52

Teacher: Student learns that the letter <u>s</u> sometimes has a <u>z</u> sound. He colors, cuts, matches and pastes the bodies of the bees onto the next page.
Those students who want to do extra work can print on the wings the same
word that is on the bee's stomach. The student may decorate the page as he
wishes.

Book I Bg.   Lesson 31 Buzzing <u>s</u>   Integral 52

Teacher: See directions on previous page.

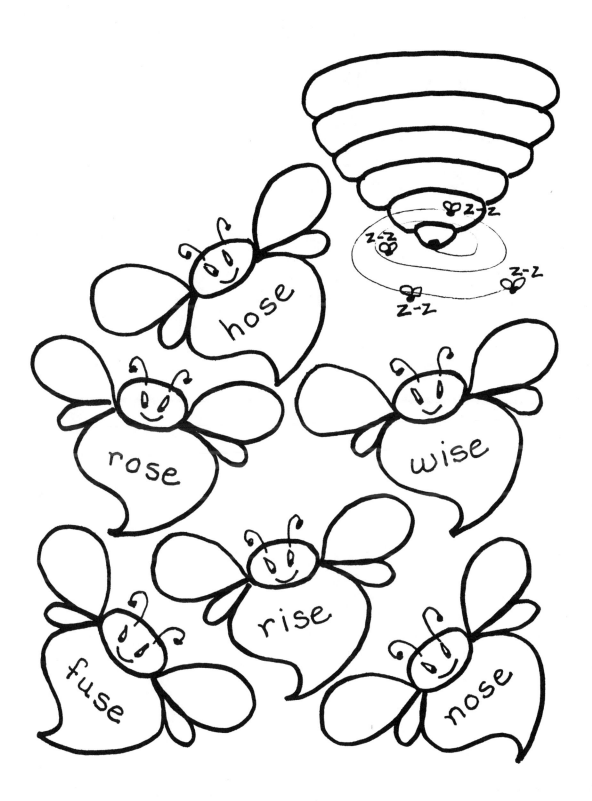

Book I Bg.   Lesson 32 Layer Cake <u>o</u>   Integral 54

Teacher: Give the Feed Words <u>does</u> and <u>have</u> to the student. He will answer
the questions <u>yes</u> or <u>no</u>. If the student gives you a reason that makes sense
to him, consider his answer correct. He makes a picture of the statement
below.

1. Does he have a hole in his nose? no yes

2. Does a sore feel fine?   no yes

3. Does a goat need a bone to eat?   no yes

4. Does a lime eat a hose?   no yes

5. Does a hose sail in the air?   no yes

6. Does a kite sail in the air?   no yes

Make a nose on a face.

Book I Bg.   Lesson 32 Layer Cake <u>i</u> and <u>o</u>   Integrals 51, 54

Teacher: Use this sheet as you did with the same type in Lesson 29. Some students will choose words like <u>side</u> because they are beginning to have the ability to manage abstractions. (The word <u>side</u> is an abstract noun.) If their answers show some logic state that you will accept their selection.

1	2	3
1. home	1. mice	1. joke
2. pine	2. tile	2. hose
3. mine	3. pole	3. hole
4. rope	4. woke	4. hope
5. life	5. rose	5. time
6. tone	6. five	6. tide

4	5	6
1. tire	1. bone	1. cone
2. code	2. dome	2. kite
3. bore	3. sore	3. cake
4. poke	4. nice	4. mole
5. fine	5. bike	5. cove
6. note	6. wife	6. tore

Book I Bg.   Lesson 32 Layer Cake <u>o</u>   Integral 54

Teacher: Student makes lines to match the words in the columns. He circles
the words in the puzzle - across and up to down only. He may cross off a
line beside the word in the column after he finds it in the puzzle. He
writes the words in the spaces below. He can decorate the page afterwards.

mole   home | | |

rose   mole | | |

home   pole | | |

pole   rose | | |

```
m  o  l  e  r  o  s  e  m
r  h  l  m  h  o  m  e  o
o  o  h  r  p  o  l  e  l
s  m  m  m  o  l  e  o  e
e  e  p  o  l  e  s  e  m
m  r  o  s  e  h  o  m  e
```

Book I Bg.   Lesson 32 <u>my</u> <u>by</u>   Integral 55

Teacher: Be sure to read the instructions in the Teacher-Student Manual
about not letting <u>i</u> hang at the end of a word. It is important for the
student to have the kinesthetic experience of changing the <u>i</u> to a <u>y</u>. Be
sure to have him draw the diagonal line onto the <u>i</u> to make the ending letter look like a <u>y</u>. Then he copies the word in the lined section. Remind
the student that <u>y</u> goes down cellar.

$$b\dot{y}$$

b i _____   m i _____

b i _____   m i _____

b i _____   m i _____

b i _____   m i _____

b i _____   m i _____

Book I Bg.   Lesson 33 z   Integral 56

Teacher: The student prints at least eight z's in each set of lines below.
Be sure he starts at the correct spot on the dotted line. Then he zooms
his first line forward as he would with a racing car. Now he puts on his
brakes, makes a line to meet the place on the floor line exactly below his
original starting point, and finishes be tracing on the floor line.

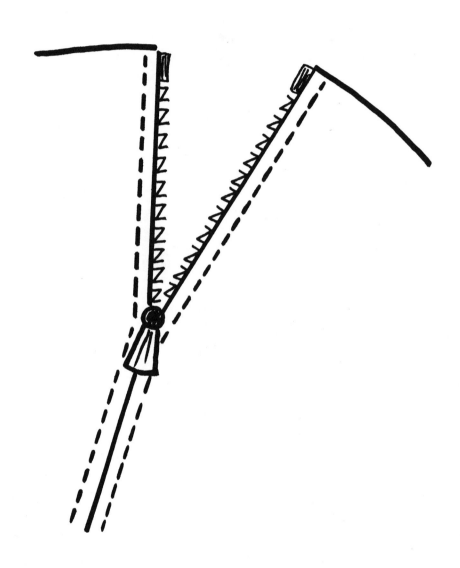

Z

Book I Bg.   Lesson 33 z   Integral 56

Teacher: Have the student print several z's on the line. Then he is to copy the words in the spaces. He can make a picture of the statement below.

z ---

size   maze   haze

_____   _____   _____
- - - - - - - -   - - - - - - - -   - - - - - - - -
_____   _____   _____

Make a rose in a vase.

Book I Bg.   Lesson 33 <u>z</u>   Integral 56

Teacher: Student underlines the words that have the letter <u>z</u> in them and copies five of them on the lines below.

see	gaze	zone	case
size	case	haze	size
wise	size	hive	gave
maze	doze	rose	zone
five	wise	maze	wise
gave	hose	case	maze
haze	maze	size	haze

Book I Bg.   Lesson 34 Layer Cake u   Integral 57

Teacher: Student colors as follows:

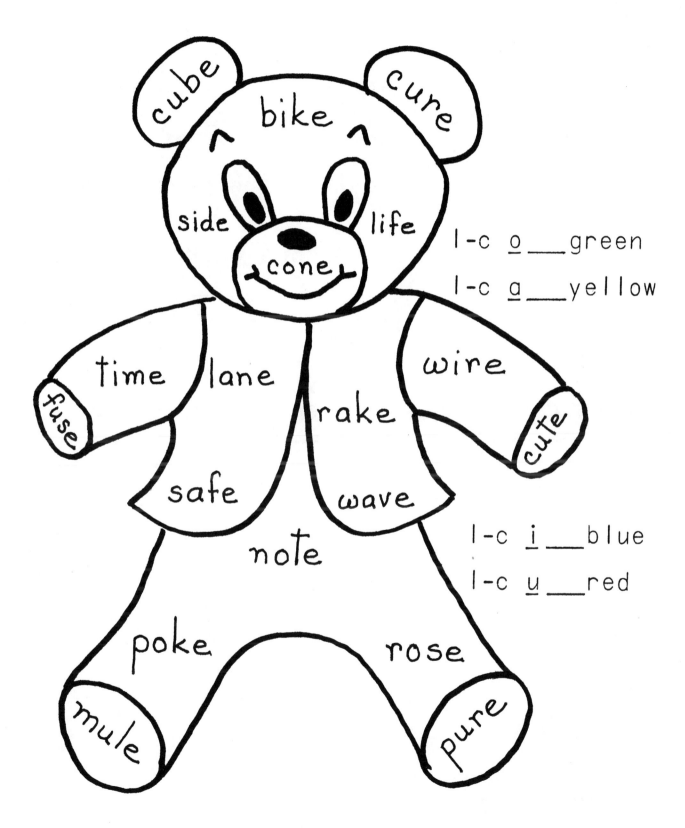

l-c <u>o</u> ___ green

l-c <u>a</u> ___ yellow

l-c <u>i</u> ___ blue

l-c <u>u</u> ___ red

Book I Bg.   Lesson 34 Layer Cake <u>u</u>   Integral 57

Teacher: The student writes <u>yes</u> or <u>no</u> to the questions (written word <u>yes</u> on the board to copy). Then he can make a picture of the statement below.

1. Can a mule make a fire? _____

2. Could a mule ride in a jeep? _____

3. Would Jake have to eat a pure lime? _____

4. Can Jake cure the sore on his heel? _____

5. Does a mule have a nose? _____

Make a mule by the side of the road.

Teacher: Student makes lines to match the words in the columns. He circles
the words in the puzzle - across and up to down only. He may cross off a
line beside the word in the column after he finds it in the puzzle. He
writes the words in the spaces below. He can decorate the page afterwards.

cute   fuse ||

cube   cute |||

fuse   pure ||

pure   cube ||

c	u	t	e	c	u	t	e	c
p	n	l	f	u	s	e	u	n
u	h	f	l	b	c	u	b	e
r	p	u	r	e	u	n	d	c
e	u	s	n	m	t	u	b	e
c	n	e	u	l	e	m	h	o

Book I Bg.   Lesson 34 Capital F   Integral 59

Teacher: Student is to print the capital F and lower case f several times
in the lines below. Then he colors the picture as directed.

Capital F___red

Fence___yellow

Flowers___orange

F f

Book I Bg.   Lesson 35 Soft g   Integral 60

Teacher: Student is told that snaky e reaches over and chews up the circle on g which makes the letter take the j sound. Student is to trace over the dotted ge in the word sage below. Then he writes sage two times. He adds ge to the other words and writes each two times. Your pupil can then color the page as he wishes.

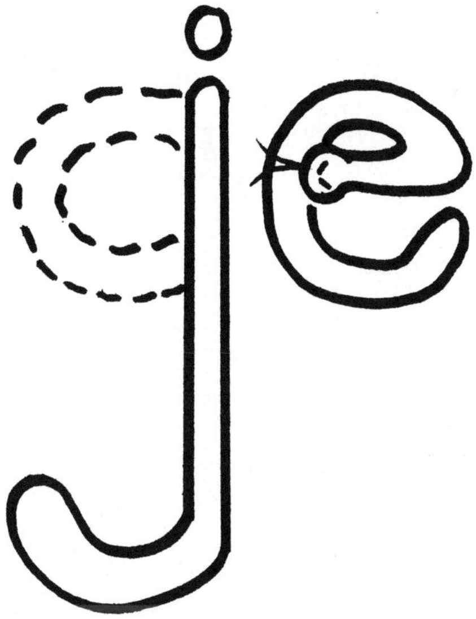

ge

j

sage		
wa		
ra		
hu		
pa		
ca		
a		

Book I Bg.   Lesson 35 Soft g   Integral 60

Teacher: Student underlines words with soft g. Remind him that the g has
the j sound if the curled up e snake is beside it. Student copies below
four of the ge words. Review the teaching of Lesson 35 in the Teacher-
Student Manual.

rage	goat	wage	gate
gave	wage	rage	wage
game	gate	page	sage
wage	haze	gate	game
goal	sage	sage	rage
sage	gaze	game	page

_____

- -

_____

Book I Bg.   Lesson 35 Soft g   Integral 60

Teacher: The puzzles from now on may have words in both directions diago-
nally (left to right and right to left), as well as, up and down and across.
Student circles the words and may cross off a line beside the word in the
column after he finds it in the puzzle. He can color the picture.

cage | | | | |

huge | | | | | |

page | | | | |

rage | | | | |

sage | | | | |

wage | | | | |

cage

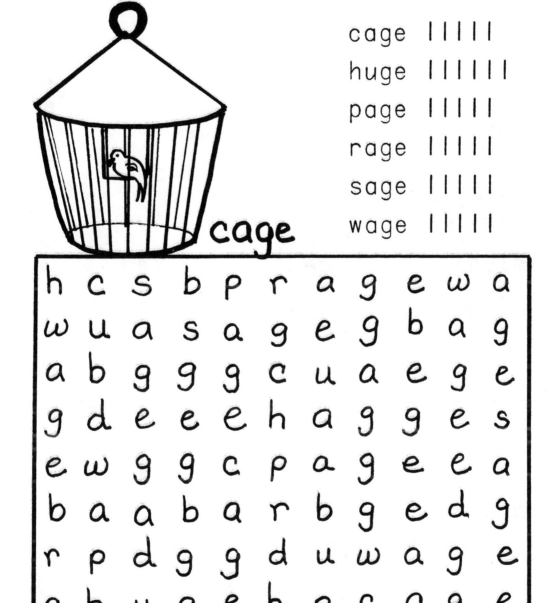

h	c	s	b	p	r	a	g	e	w	a
w	u	a	s	a	g	e	g	b	a	g
a	b	g	g	g	c	u	a	e	g	e
g	d	e	e	e	h	a	g	g	e	s
e	w	g	g	c	p	a	g	e	e	a
b	a	a	b	a	r	b	g	e	d	g
r	p	d	g	g	d	u	w	a	g	e
a	h	u	g	e	h	p	c	a	g	e
g	p	a	g	e	u	r	a	g	e	a
e	c	a	g	e	g	h	u	g	e	g
d	s	a	g	e	e	w	a	g	e	e

Book I Bg.   Lesson 36 Open Layer Cake Words A   Integrals 61-65

Teacher: See directions in Lesson 10. Student reads the words in the first
list and puts x's beside six open layer cake words. He prints these on the
illustrated open layer cake page. At another time, he follows the same procedure with the second list.

Day 1

ice	pole	weed
oar	eat	oak
Eve	ape	soap
mice	ace	tea
maid	cure	use

Day 2

seed	roar	Abe
ate	Eve	bite
oat	mole	age
mule	ear	sail
ice	use	sea

Book I Bg.   Open Layer Cake Words   Integrals 62-65

Teacher: Student uses this page with open layer cake words. With the arrow
pointed away from his stomach, he puts the letters in the correct spaces of
the cake. He then prints the word twice in the spaces below the picture.

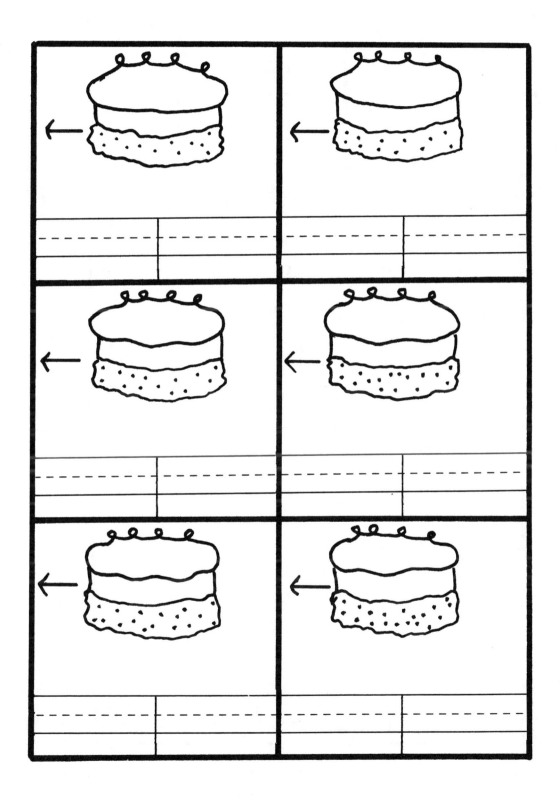

Book I Bg.   Lesson 36 Open Layer Cake Words <u>A</u>   Integrals 61-65

Teacher: Student circles the words and may cross off a line beside the
word in the column after he finds it in the puzzle.

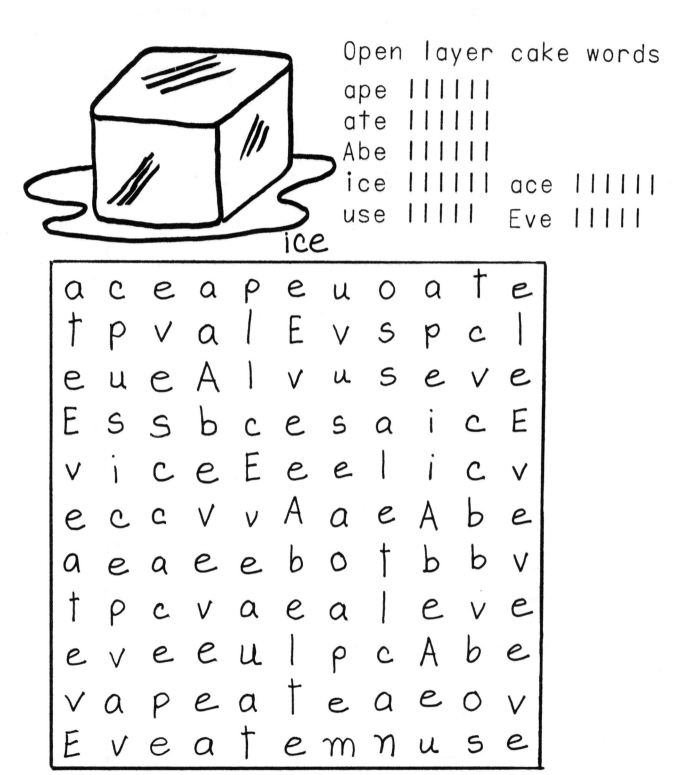

Open layer cake words

ape ||||||
ate ||||||
Abe ||||||
ice |||||| ace ||||||
use ||||| Eve |||||

ice

a	c	e	a	p	e	u	o	a	t	e
t	p	v	a	l	E	v	s	p	c	l
e	u	e	A	l	v	u	s	e	v	e
E	s	s	b	c	e	s	a	i	c	E
v	i	c	e	E	e	e	l	i	c	v
e	c	c	v	v	A	a	e	A	b	e
a	e	a	e	e	b	o	t	b	b	v
t	p	c	v	a	e	a	l	e	v	e
e	v	e	e	u	l	p	c	A	b	e
v	a	p	e	a	t	e	a	e	o	v
E	v	e	a	t	e	m	n	u	s	e

Book I Bg.   Lesson 36 Open Layer Cake Words <u>A</u>   Integrals 61-65

Teacher: The student puts an <u>x</u> beside each <u>open layer cake</u> word (not the open peanut butter and jelly words). He then copies those words he selects on the lines below.

oak	mule	eel	Mike
ate	ace	seal	Eve
gear	pine	ice	use
hope	paid	sail	Abe
age	ape	rice	nose

Book I Bg.   Lesson 36 Capital <u>A</u>   Integral 61

Teacher: The student finds and colors the capital <u>A</u> in the picture. He is to print the capital <u>A</u> and lower case <u>a</u> several times in the lines below. Then he can decorate the page as he wishes.

A a

Book I Bg.   Lesson 37 Review P+J and L-C Words   Integrals 6, 17, 20, 21,
                                                          49, 51, 54, 57

Teacher: Student makes lines to match the words in the columns. He circles
the words in the puzzle - across and up to down only. He may cross off a
line beside the word in the column after he finds it in the puzzle. He
writes the words in the spaces below. He can decorate the page afterwards.

read	nail II
gate	pile III
nail	read II
foam	cube III
pile	gate II
cube	foam II

m	n	g	n	a	i	l	f	h
r	e	a	d	f	p	i	l	e
e	n	t	f	o	a	m	f	c
a	a	e	g	a	t	e	c	u
d	i	l	n	m	u	n	u	b
f	l	h	u	n	c	u	b	e
p	i	l	e	p	i	l	e	c

Book I Bg.   Lesson 37 Review P+J and L-C Words   Integrals 6, 17, 20,
                                                            21, 49, 51, 54, 57

Teacher: See directions in Lesson 10. Student reads the words in the first
list and puts x's beside three peanut butter and jelly words and three layer
cake words. He prints these on the illustrated peanut butter and jelly and
layer cake page. At another time, he follows the same procedure with the
second list.

Day 1

cone	tail	ear
oak	air	seed
sea	mine	ate
foam	ace	eel
ice	use	face

Day 2

tea	cure	use
read	ape	sea
bite	aid	sale
age	ice	eat
oar	leak	soap

Name -- Date ------------

Book I Bg.   Peanut Butter and Jelly and Layer Cake Words   Integrals 6, 17,
                                                                20, 21, 49, 51, 54, 57

Teacher: Student uses this page with peanut butter and jelly words as well as
layer cake words. With the arrow pointed away from his stomach, he puts the
letters in the correct spaces of the sandwich or cake. He then prints the word
twice in the spaces below the picture.

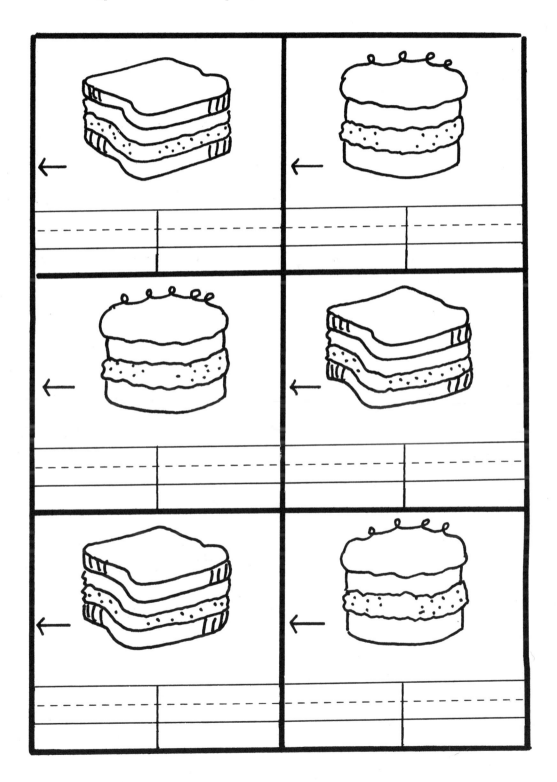

Book I Bg.   Lesson 38 Review Open Sandwich and Open Layer Cake Words
                                        Integrals 33-36, 38, 39, 62-65

Teacher: See directions in Lesson 10. Student reads the words in the first
list and puts x's beside two of each kind of open sandwich words and two
open layer cake words. He prints these on the illustrated open sandwich and
open layer cake page. At another time, he follows the same procedure with
the second list.

Day 1

ace	sea	name
bee	read	ice
need	hike	side
oak	tail	aim
pail	seed	hope

Day 2

use	wire	rate
face	bone	aid
cube	eel	bite
tea	ape	feed
bean	lace	see

Book I Bg.   Open Sandwich and Open Layer Cake Words   Integrals 33-36, 38, 39, 62-65

Teacher: Student uses this page with both kinds of open sandwich words as well as open layer cake words. Make sure that the student has the arrow pointed away from his stomach as he starts each new word. The student puts the letters in the correct spaces of the sandwich or cake. He then prints the word twice in the spaces below the picture.

Book I Bg.   Lesson 38 Review Open Sandwich Words   Integrals 33-36

Teacher: Student makes lines to match the words in the columns. He circles
the words in the puzzle - across and up to down only. He may cross off a
line beside the word in the column after he finds it in the puzzle. He
writes the words in the spaces below. He can decorate the page afterwards.

oar	eel |||
eat	ear |||
oat	oak ||||
eel	oar ||||||
oak	oat ||||||
ear	eat ||||

```
o  a  r  o  a  r  o  a  k
a  e  o  a  r  e  a  t  e
t  e  a  t  o  a  t  e  a
e  l  k  e  a  r  o  a  t
a  a  r  e  r  o  a  r  l
t  e  e  l  o  a  k  t  h
```

Book I Bg.   Lesson 38 Review Open Layer Cake Words   Integrals 62-65

Teacher: Student makes lines to match the words in the columns. He circles
the words in the puzzle - across and up to down only. He may cross off a
line beside the word in the column after he finds it in the puzzle. He
writes the words in the spaces below. He can decorate the page afterwards.

ace	ice |||
use	ate ||||||
ice	ace ||||
Eve	use ||||
ate	Eve |||

a	c	E	v	e	i	c	e	u
t	u	a	c	e	c	i	c	s
e	s	t	a	a	e	u	s	e
v	e	e	l	c	i	s	a	a
a	t	E	v	e	c	e	t	t
a	c	e	a	t	E	v	e	e

Book I Bg.   Lesson 39 Review Open Sandwich and Open Layer Cake Words
                          Integrals 33-36, 38, 39, 62-65

Teacher: Student writes in the lined spaces the words that match the pictures.

eel   see   oak leaf
ice cube   bee   oat meal

Book I Bg.   Lesson 39 Review <u>no go so</u> <u>he me</u> ai=ay Integrals 14, 27, 48

Teacher: The student is to write the following words correctly after you have reviewed the concepts of <u>noa</u>=<u>no</u> (Lesson 8), <u>hea</u>=<u>he</u> (Lesson 18), and ai=ay (Lesson 28).

bai		mai	
dai		lai	
mi		mea	
goa		soa	
sai		wea	
hea		Kai	
wai		noa	
bi		Jai	
hai		pai	
wea		rai	

Book I Bg.   Lesson 40 <u>bl</u>   Integral 66

Teacher: Student underlines the beginning sounds as follows: (Student can do one or more columns a day. Those with severe problems may need to do only <u>bl</u> one day, <u>b</u> the next, etc.)

bl___blue   b___green   d___yellow

1.	2.	3.	4.
bleed	dear	beat	base
bale	bean	deal	blaze
base	blade	beam	deer
blame	beef	bleak	bleat
boat	blare	beak	bleed
dare	beak	bleed	bone
bake	blaze	blade	date
dice	dare	blare	bleak
blare	bleat	dare	beak
bean	deer	blaze	dear

Book I Bg.   Lesson 40 <u>bl</u>   Integral 66

Teacher: Student circles the words. He may cross off a line beside the word in the column after he finds it in the puzzle. He can color the picture.

blaze

blade | | |
blame | | |
blare | | |
blaze | | |
bleak | | |
bleat | | |
bleed | | |

b	l	a	d	e	b	l	e	a	t	l
l	l	h	b	n	k	b	l	a	m	e
a	h	e	d	a	l	d	e	d	b	h
m	b	h	e	d	b	l	a	z	e	b
e	d	l	h	d	b	l	e	a	k	d
d	b	h	a	b	d	d	a	h	n	g
b	l	b	b	r	a	h	n	r	m	b
l	e	l	b	l	e	a	t	n	e	l
e	e	a	b	h	a	b	l	a	d	e
a	d	r	b	l	a	z	e	b	d	e
k	h	e	b	l	a	m	e	h	l	d

Book I Bg.   Lesson 40 Capital <u>B</u>   Integral 67

Teacher: Student traces the capital <u>B</u> in the picture and then prints several
<u>B</u>'s in the lines below. The picture can be colored.

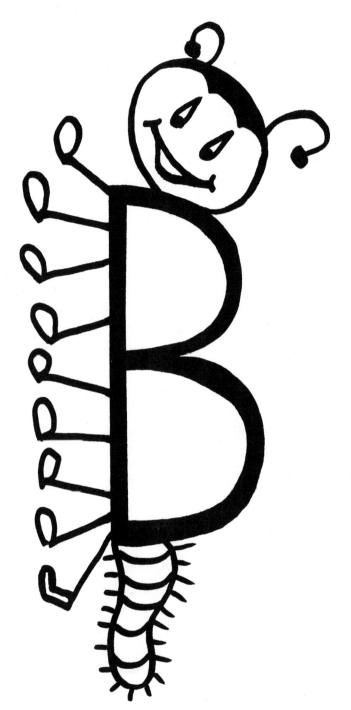

B b

Teacher: Student makes lines to match the words.

blade	broke	blaze	braid
brain	blare	braid	brine
bleed	blade	bride	blaze
blare	bleed	blame	bride
broke	brain	brine	blame

brain	bleed	blare	brace
bride	broke	brace	bleak
brine	brain	bride	blare
bleed	bride	bleed	bride
broke	brine	bleak	bleed

bleak	bleed	brace	base
breed	beak	broke	bale
beak	beat	base	blade
bleed	bleak	blade	brace
beat	breed	bale	broke

Book I Bg.   Lesson 41 <u>br</u>   Integral 68

Teacher: This sheet is to be used for two separate days. The first day
is an underlining procedure. The second day the student puts colored <u>x</u>'s
beside the words as directed.

Day 1:   Day 2:

bl___blue   Beside p+j___purple <u>x</u>

br___brown   Beside l-c___yellow <u>x</u>

braid   blare   Blake

blame   blaze   blade

bean   broke   bore

dear   bean   beat

date   brine   brain

bride   bleak   brake

bleed   brave   brace

Teacher: See directions in Lesson 35.

←braid

brace | | | | breeze | | |
braid | | | bride | | |
brain | | | brine | |
brake | | broke | |
brave | |

b	r	a	c	e	d	b	r	o	k	e
r	r	b	n	b	b	r	e	e	z	e
a	b	e	r	b	r	i	n	e	b	b
i	l	r	e	a	o	a	m	u	r	r
d	b	h	a	z	k	h	c	n	a	i
h	b	r	a	v	e	e	m	e	c	d
b	r	a	i	d	e	u	n	h	e	e
b	r	a	i	d	b	r	a	i	n	m
d	b	r	a	i	n	b	r	i	d	e
h	b	r	a	k	e	b	r	a	c	e
b	r	e	e	z	e	b	r	a	i	n

Book I Bg.   Lesson 42 <u>cl</u>   Integral 69

Teacher: Student colors as follows:

clear___green   claim___red

clean___yellow   close___blue

cloak___orange

clear	cloak	close	close	clean	clear
clean	claim	clean	cloak	claim	cloak
close	cloak	clear	clear	clean	close
close	clean	clear	clear	cloak	close
cloak	claim	cloak	clean	claim	clean
clear	clean	close	close	cloak	clear

Book I Bg.   Lesson 42 <u>cl</u>   Integral 69

Teacher: Remind your students that <u>p</u>eanut butter and <u>j</u>elly will be written
as p+j. Layer <u>c</u>ake words will be l-c. Stress these first letter sounds.
Students are to underline the blends as follows. (Those with severe problems should do only <u>one</u> blend per day.) Fill the colors in so the students
will not guess at the words.

Day 1:   Day 2:

bl___blue   Beside p+j___purple <u>x</u>

br___brown   Beside l-c___yellow <u>x</u>

cl___red

braid   clove   bride

clear   brave   blare

clean   beef   clear

brake   cloak   brine

bean   blame   clove

claim   clear   breed

brace   blade   clean

Book I Bg.   Lesson 42 <u>cl</u>   Integral 69

Teacher: Student circles the words. He may cross off a line beside the
word in the column after he finds it in the puzzle. He can color the picture.

claim |||
Claire |||
clean |||
clear |||
cloak |||
close |||

Claire

c	l	a	i	m	n	e	b	h	n	e
l	l	h	b	n	r	m	h	n	r	b
o	h	e	d	i	C	l	a	i	r	e
s	c	d	a	b	c	n	a	h	b	c
e	h	l	d	n	a	l	n	m	h	l
c	C	c	e	e	C	l	o	s	e	a
l	l	c	l	a	i	m	n	a	h	i
e	o	c	l	e	r	n	u	m	k	m
a	a	d	b	o	a	c	l	o	a	k
n	k	h	l	d	s	r	h	b	d	n
c	l	e	a	r	n	e	m	n	r	h

Book I Bg.   Lesson 43 <u>cr</u>   Integral 70

Teacher: Student colors as follows:

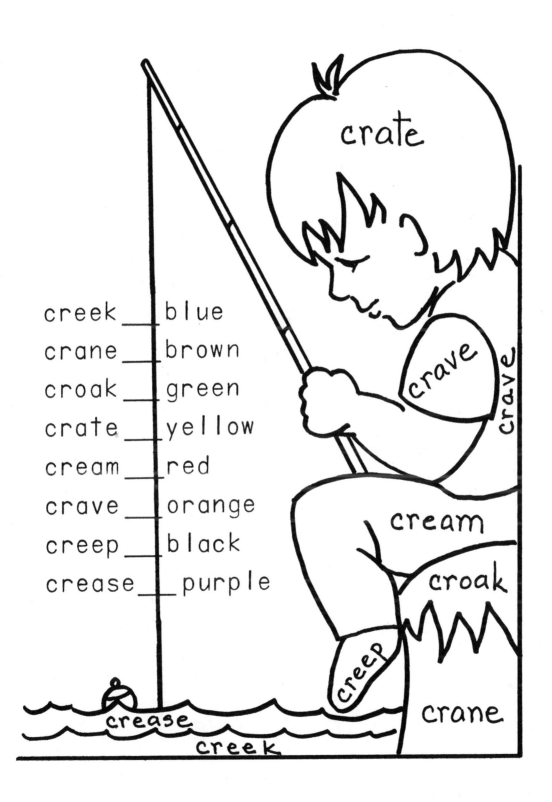

creek___blue
crane___brown
croak___green
crate___yellow
cream___red
crave___orange
creep___black
crease___purple

Book I Bg.   Lesson 43 <u>cr</u>   Integral 70

Teacher: Student circles the words. He may cross off a line beside the word in the column after he finds it in the puzzle. He can color the picture.

Craig II

crane III   crease II

crate II   creek IIII

crave II   creep II

cream II   croak III

```
c r a n e n h b c g c
c r e e k u r d r c r
c r e a m n h r a r o
r c r e e p c m n e a
a h r n k h c r e e k
i C r a i g r s o p d
g c o n v b a d m a b
c r a t e e t a n u k
c a h c r e e k h d b
m n u c c r a v e h n
n e n h c r e a s e m
```

Book I Bg.   Lesson 43 <u>buy</u>   Integral 71

Teacher: Keep reviewing the fact that <u>by</u> and <u>buy</u> sound the same, but the word meaning <u>to purchase</u> has that silent <u>u</u> in it. We pretend the <u>u</u> is a container to hold the bag of whatever we <u>buy</u>. The student prints the word <u>buy</u> three times. He can then decorate the page as he wishes.

Book I Bg.   Lesson 43 <u>buy</u>   Integral 71

Teacher: Be sure to explain that <u>by</u> tells where <u>I</u> am (position), whereas,
<u>buy</u> has the letter <u>u</u> in the word which acts as a container to hold the bag
of whatever you <u>buy</u>. Tell the student he is to help the bee go <u>down</u> to the
hive by copying each word in the next space.

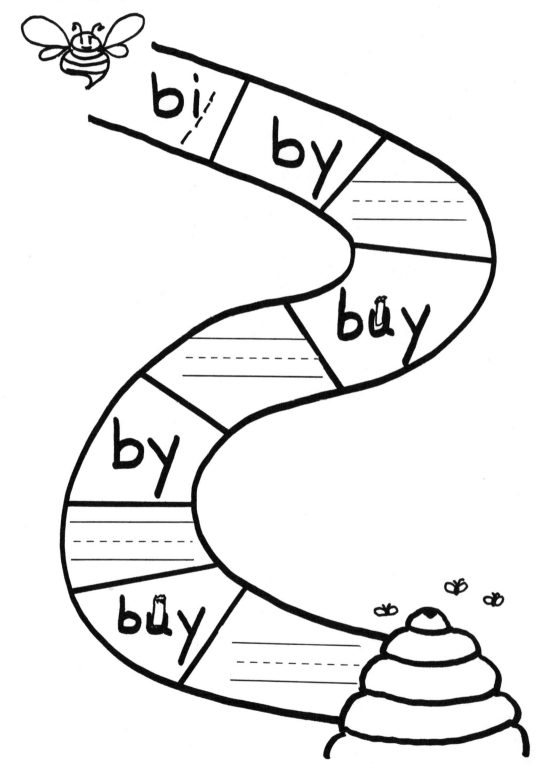

Book I Bg.   Lesson 43 <u>cr</u> <u>but</u> <u>buy</u>   Integrals 70, 71

Teacher: Student writes <u>yes</u> or <u>no</u>.

1. I can buy a pile of rice. _____

2. Craig can bleed. _____

3. Clive Crane can close the gate. _____

4. Craig can creep in the cave. _____

5. The crane can buy a lake. _____

Name _____ Date _____

1. Mike can buy the cream. _____

2. Cream makes the jeep go. _____

3. Cream is nice on meat. _____

4. I can buy a crate. _____

5. I can buy <u>cream</u>, but I can<u>not</u> buy a
   week. _____

Book I Bg.   Lesson 44 dr   Integral 72

Teacher: Student colors as follows:

drake___brown   drape___orange
drone___purple   drain___red
drove___orange   drive___blue
dream___yellow

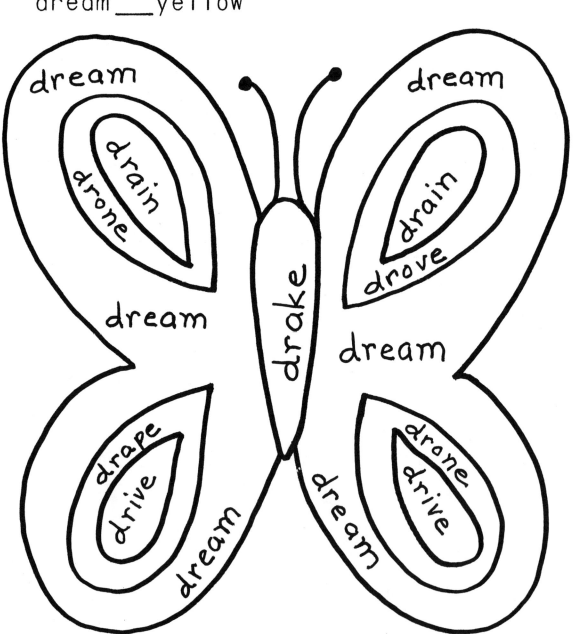

Book I Bg.   Lesson 44 <u>you</u>   Integral 73

Teacher: Point out the fact that here is another word with a silent letter.
To say the word <u>you</u>, one has to sound out the <u>y</u> and add the long <u>u</u> sound.
Wouldn't it be nice if we could spell the word <u>you</u> as just one letter <u>u</u>? We
use one letter for <u>I</u>! Student prints the word <u>you</u> three times and then colors.

Book I Bg.   Lesson 44 <u>dr</u> <u>you</u>   Integrals 72, 73

Teacher: See directions in Lesson 19.

1. Can you clean the ⬜ ?

2. Craig could ⬜ you to the creek.

3. Is the drain ⬜ ?

4. Could a ⬜ seem real?

5. Would you like to have a crane and a
   ⬜ ?

6. He ⬜ the jeep to the lake.

- -

| dream | drake | drive | dry | drain | drove |

Book I Bg.   Lesson 44 <u>dr</u>   Integral 72

Teacher: Student circles the words. He may cross off a line beside the
word in the column after he finds it in the puzzle. He can color the picture.

drive

drain | | |
drake | | |
drape | | |
dream | | |
drive | | |
drone | | |
drove | | |

```
d r a i n m d r i v e
r r d r a k e n u d d
e d i r d d b m d r r
a n r v a r n n r a a
m h n o e i o u a k p
n u m v v v n v k e e
b d o d r e a m e d d
d r a p e g b p n r r
d o b d r e a m u a o
h n m u d r o n e i n
n e h n d r a i n n e
```

Teacher: Student colors as follows:

fleet___purple   flake___yellow

float___orange   flee ___red

flare___blue   flame___green

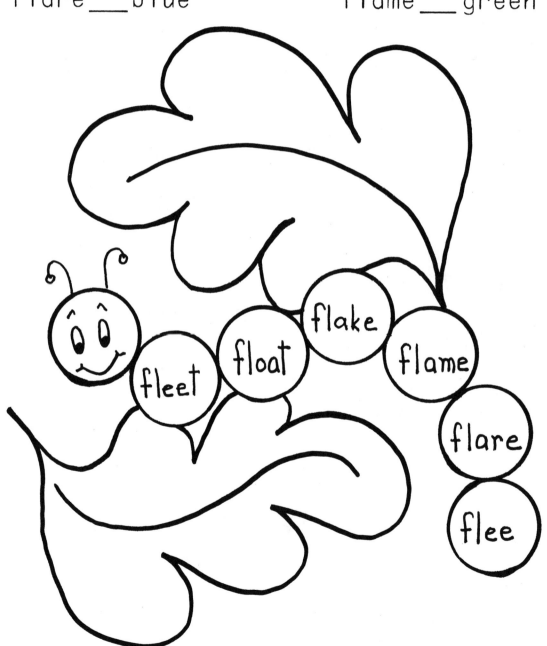

Book I Bg.   Lesson 45 <u>fl</u>   Integral 74

Teacher: Give the directions in Lesson 29. Students can do one or two
columns a day and copy below the words they select.

1	2	3	4
cream	fleet	blame	drake
flame	fly	bride	cloak
dream	blade	brine	flare
drive	blame	crate	crane
rain	bleed	drain	blaze
flake	brace	bean	fear
braid	flea	deal	feet

Book I Bg.   Lesson 45 <u>fl</u>   Integral 74

Teacher: Student circles the words. He may cross off a line beside the word in the column after he finds it in the puzzle. He can color the picture.

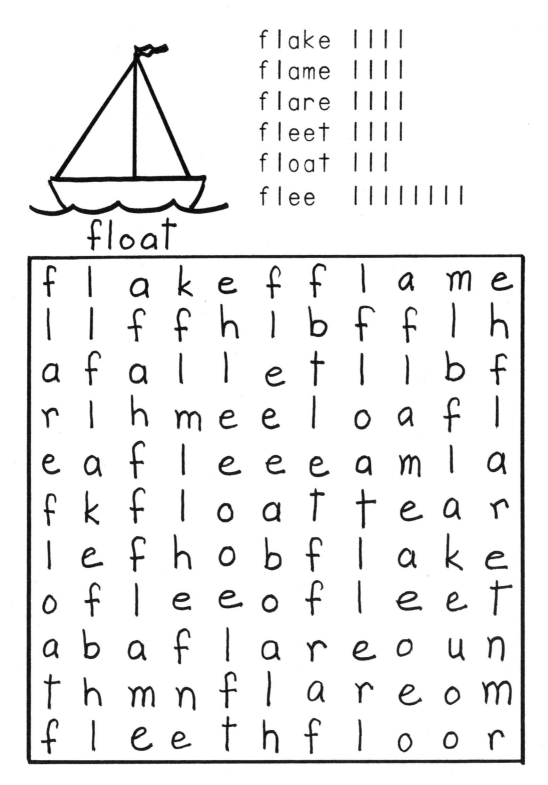

flake ||||
flame ||||
flare ||||
fleet ||||
float |||
flee ||||||||

float

f	l	a	k	e	f	f	l	a	m	e
l	l	f	f	h	l	b	f	f	l	h
a	f	a	l	l	e	t	l	l	b	f
r	l	h	m	e	e	l	o	a	f	l
e	a	f	l	e	e	e	a	m	l	a
f	k	f	l	o	a	t	t	e	a	r
l	e	f	h	o	b	f	l	a	k	e
o	f	l	e	e	o	f	l	e	e	t
a	b	a	f	l	a	r	e	o	u	n
t	h	m	n	f	l	a	r	e	o	m
f	l	e	e	t	h	f	l	o	o	r

Name ------------------------------ **Date** ----------

Book I Bg.   Lesson 45 eye   Integral 75

Teacher: Student completes the two pictures by incorporating the word <u>eye</u>
into the eyes and nose. He then writes the word <u>eye</u> six times in the lines
below. He can decorate the page as he wishes.

Book I Bg.   Lesson 46 <u>fr</u>   Integral 76

Teacher: Student colors as follows: (Explain that tan can be made by using brown lightly.)

from___yellow   froze___brown
freak___orange   frame___black
free___tan

Book I Bg.   Lesson 46 <u>fr</u>   Integral 76

Teacher: Student circles the words. He may cross off a line beside the
word in the column after he finds it in the puzzle. He can draw a picture
in the frame. In Lesson 49 the student will learn that <u>freeze</u> is a p+j
word. The letter <u>z</u> in long vowel words always sticks to <u>e</u>. He will also
find that <u>e</u> sticks to some words that end in <u>s</u>, <u>v</u>, or <u>c</u>.

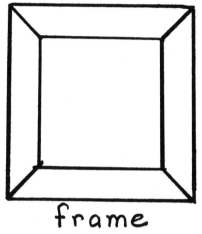

frame

frame | | | | |

freak | | | |

freeze | | | | |

froze | | | | |

free | | | | | | | | | | |

f	r	a	m	e	f	r	e	e	z	e
r	r	f	r	o	z	e	f	r	e	e
o	f	e	r	f	r	a	m	e	h	e
z	f	r	e	a	k	f	f	f	e	n
e	h	e	a	z	m	r	n	r	u	f
f	r	e	e	m	e	e	f	e	e	r
f	r	e	e	z	e	e	h	e	b	e
r	n	u	n	z	f	r	o	z	e	a
e	m	h	o	n	r	f	r	e	a	k
a	f	r	a	m	e	f	r	o	z	e
k	f	h	f	r	e	e	z	e	n	u

Book I Bg.   Lesson 46 <u>from</u>   Integral 77

Teacher: Student prints <u>on</u> and <u>om</u> on the right side.   Then he prints the
word <u>from</u> three times on each line.

on

om

from

Book I Bg.   Lesson 47 <u>gl</u>   Integral 78

Teacher: Student circles the words. He may cross off a line beside the
word in the column after he finds it in the puzzle. He can color the picture.

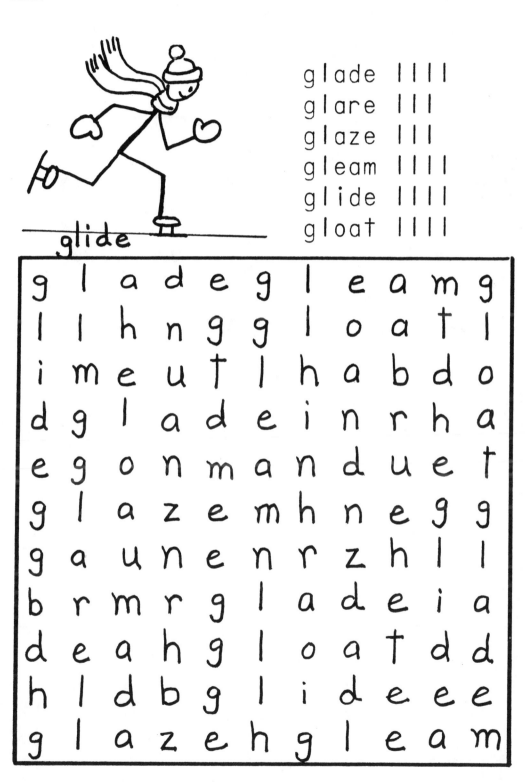

glade | | | |
glare | | |
glaze | | |
gleam | | | |
glide | | | |
gloat | | | |

glide

g	l	a	d	e	g	l	e	a	m	g
l	l	h	n	g	g	l	o	a	t	l
i	m	e	u	t	l	h	a	b	d	o
d	g	l	a	d	e	i	n	r	h	a
e	g	o	n	m	a	n	d	u	e	t
g	l	a	z	e	m	h	n	e	g	g
g	a	u	n	e	n	r	z	h	l	l
b	r	m	r	g	l	a	d	e	i	a
d	e	a	h	g	l	o	a	t	d	d
h	l	d	b	g	l	i	d	e	e	e
g	l	a	z	e	h	g	l	e	a	m

Book I Bg.   Lesson 47 <u>cr</u> vs. <u>gr</u>   Integrals 70, 79

Teacher: This page can be used for two days. Review the sounds of <u>c</u> vs. <u>g</u>
(Lesson I Parts 3 and 4). Tell the student he is to read the words and de-
cide whether the first sound is <u>up</u> in the mouth or <u>down</u> in the throat. He is
to copy the words with the mouth sound under the picture <u>without</u> the neck and
copy the words with the throat sound under the picture <u>with</u> the neck. After
the second day's work the student can decorate the pictures. These directions
are difficult for some. Take a small group at a time through the first two
words and get them to make the decisions.

1	2	Day 1	Day 2	1	2
		groan	gripe		
		croak	creep		
		gain	creak		
		crane	coat		
		cream	grade		
		grave	grime		
		crave	creek		
		grain	came		
		cane	grape		
		groan	grope		

Book I Bg.   Lesson 47 <u>gr</u>   Integral 79

Teacher: Student circles the words. He may cross off a line beside the
word in the column after he finds it in the puzzle. He can color the grass
green.

green

grade	II	green	II
grain	I	greet	II
grave	II	grime	II
graze	II	gripe	II
grease	I	groan	II
greed	II	grove	II

```
g r a d e h g r a z e
r r g r e e d g b h n
i h e n t g g r a d e
m n u e g r o a n u g
e h e b d e h v g n r
g r e a s e n e r h o
g r a i n n p u e g v
r n u g r i p e e r e
i h b g r o v e t a n
m d n g r o a n h z u
e g r a v e g r e e n
```

Book I Bg.   Lesson 47 <u>gl</u> <u>gr</u>   Integrals 78, 79

Teacher: Student colors as follows:
(These directives are difficult for some. Patiently repeat the directions
as the child proceeds.)

<u>gl</u> + p+j___blue   <u>gr</u> + p+j___red

<u>gl</u> + l-c___yellow   <u>gr</u> + l-c___green

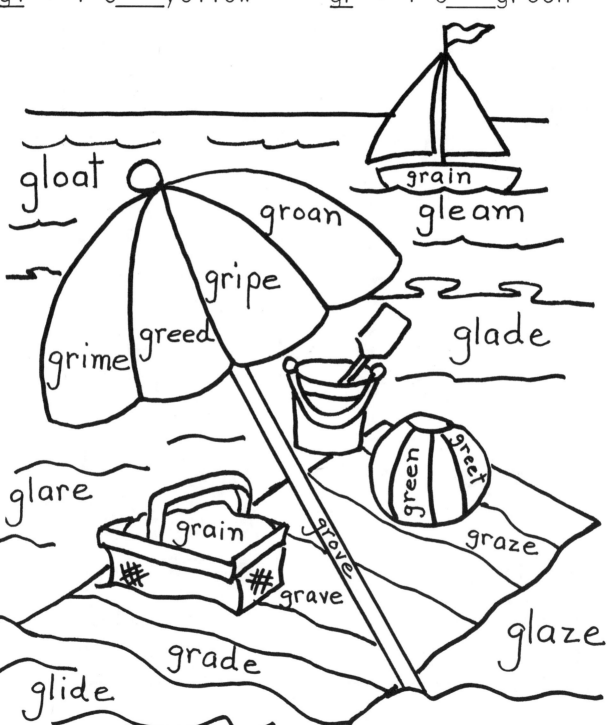

Teacher: This is an exercise for students needing the speech correction for <u>pl</u>. Students who do not have this problem can do the exercise to help them become aware that some people's tongues play tricks and make the person place the tongue in the wrong place. Explain to the student that he is to put <u>x</u>'s in the pictures where the person has the wrong tongue placement for <u>pl</u>. He is to print <u>pw</u> in those frames and <u>pl</u> in the pictures with the correct tongue placement. He can then decorate the pictures.

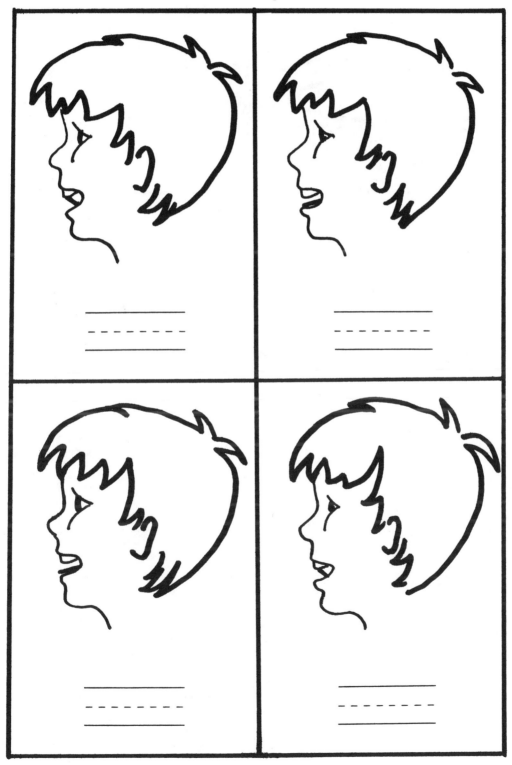

Book I Bg.   Lesson 48 <u>pl</u>   Integral 80

Teacher: Student circles the words. He may cross off a line beside the word in the column after he finds it in the puzzle. He can color the picture. Notice that the letter <u>y</u> in the puzzle has a curl on the tail. In the future there will be deviations in some of the printing so that the student can begin to handle a variety of type faces.

plain ||||
plane |||||
plate |||
play ||||||
plead |||||
please |||
plea |||||||

plate

p	l	a	n	e	p	l	a	y	y	b
l	l	p	l	a	n	e	h	a	b	d
a	h	e	l	i	h	p	l	e	a	d
n	p	p	a	a	u	p	l	e	n	e
e	b	l	l	d	y	b	l	a	t	l
p	p	a	e	a	h	p	p	a	i	b
l	l	t	b	a	y	n	l	d	i	n
e	a	e	u	a	s	p	a	a	u	n
a	t	p	l	a	n	e	i	b	y	h
s	e	p	h	p	l	a	n	e	d	r
e	r	u	n	p	l	e	a	s	e	h

Book I Bg.   Lesson 48 <u>pr</u>   Integral 81

Teacher: Student circles the words. He may cross off a line beside the
word in the column after he finds it in the puzzle. He can color the picture.

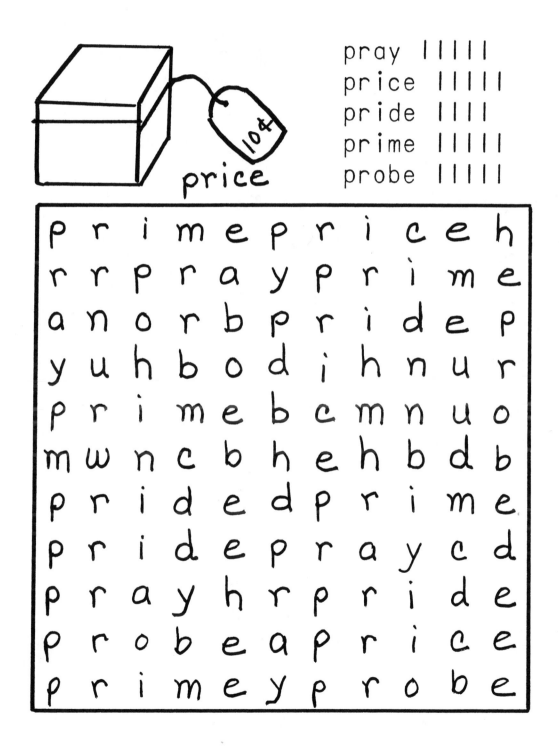

pray | | | | |
price | | | | |
pride | | | |
prime | | | | |
probe | | | | |

price

p	r	i	m	e	p	r	i	c	e	h
r	r	p	r	a	y	p	r	i	m	e
a	n	o	r	b	p	r	i	d	e	p
y	u	h	b	o	d	i	h	n	u	r
p	r	i	m	e	b	c	m	n	u	o
m	w	n	c	b	h	e	h	b	d	b
p	r	i	d	e	d	p	r	i	m	e
p	r	i	d	e	p	r	a	y	c	d
p	r	a	y	h	r	p	r	i	d	e
p	r	o	b	e	a	p	r	i	c	e
p	r	i	m	e	y	p	r	o	b	e

Teacher: Student colors as follows:

<u>pl</u> + p+j___red   <u>pr</u> + p+j___green
<u>pl</u> + l-c___blue   <u>pr</u> + l-c___yellow

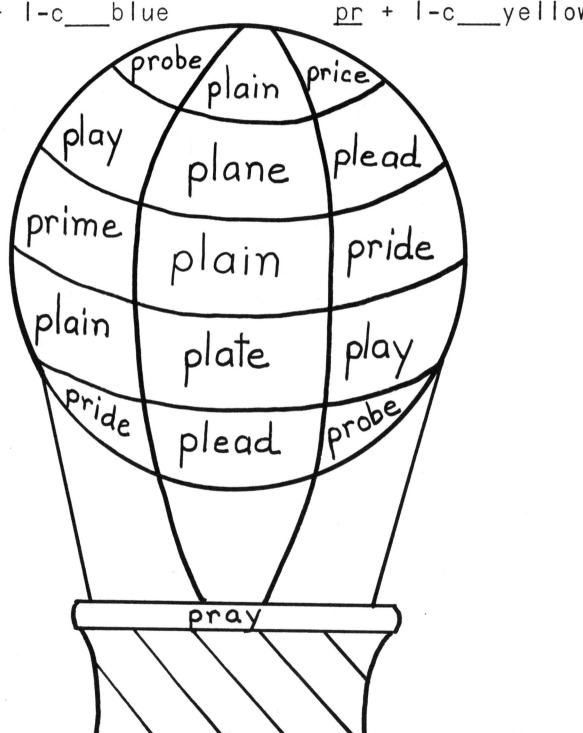

Book I Bg.   Lesson 48 <u>your</u>   Integral 82

Teacher: Student sounds out <u>y</u>, colors the silent <u>o</u> circle yellow, pronounces
the <u>u</u>. Student writes <u>you</u> three times. Student repeats the procedure for
the second picture and adds the <u>sound</u> of <u>r</u>. He writes <u>your</u> three times.

Book I Bg.   Lesson 49 <u>ve</u> <u>ze</u> <u>se</u> <u>ce</u>   Integral 83

Teacher: The student is taught that p+j and layer cake words (singular) end-
ing in the letters <u>v</u> <u>z</u> <u>s</u> <u>c</u> grab <u>e</u>. Student is to put an <u>e</u> at the end of the
words in the columns that need this letter.

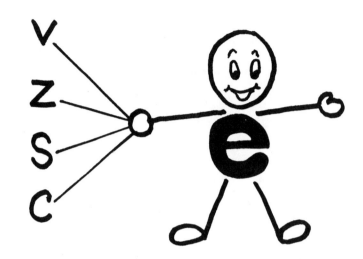

pleas	doz	weep	breez
plead	fleec	seal	leaf
weav	teas	haz	leap
weed	freez	creak	peep
froz	leav	bean	ros
creas	craz	maz	haz
heav	crav	greas	brav
peac	lean	gear	prais

Book I Bg.   Lesson 49 <u>ve</u> <u>ze</u> <u>se</u> <u>ce</u>   Integral 83

Teacher: Student is to add <u>e</u> after long vowel words ending in <u>v</u>, <u>z</u>, <u>s</u>, <u>c</u>.
The child needs these letters in front of him until he has practiced this
type of activity often.

Z V S C

plead	weav	pleas
creas	pleas	craz
peac	greas	lean
froz	fleec	creas
peep	peac	weep
teas	breez	weav
freez	creas	freez
heav	leav	teas
creek	teas	fleec
breez	haz	leav
greas	froz	peac
gear	creas	breed
green	weak	breez

Book I Bg.   Lesson 50 <u>sl</u>   Integral 84

Teacher: Many students consider this type of page exhausting. You can whet their appetites by telling them that there will be some very silly questions. Can they find them? Mark <u>x</u>'s beside the numbers of the sentences that are silly.

1. Could a m<u>on</u>ster slice a bean? _____

2. Would you eat your meat with slime on it? _____

3. Could you slide on a slope? _____

4. Could a seat smile? _____

5. Could sleet be like rain that freeze<u>s</u>? _____

1. Would you sleep on the ice? _____

2. Can you slide in the breezy air? _____

3. Would Mike eat gravy on bee<u>ts</u>? _____

4. Can you slice a loaf? _____

5. Does a toad seem sleepy to you? _____

1. Does the mean m<u>on</u>ster <u>like to</u> smear grease on your sleeve? --------

2. Have you <u>seen a</u> smile on the face of a goat? --------

3. Have you seen smoke in the <u>firep</u>lace? --------

4. Have you seen a drake smile? --------

5. If you <u>freeze.</u> would it make you sneeze? ---------

Name ------------------------------------- Date ----------

1. Would Craig <u>smear</u> grease on the feet of a deer? --------

2. Could smoke slide from a fire? --------

3. Would <u>you</u> smear grease on your green coat? ---------

4. Would I be crazy to smoke? --------

5. Can you clean the <u>smear</u> of grease from your plate? --------

Book I Bg.   Lesson 50 <u>sl</u> <u>sm</u> <u>sn</u>   Integrals 84-86

1. Craig can _____ if he sleep<u>s</u>.
   sneak   snore   snail

2. A _____ can hide in his home.
   smear   sneak   snail

3. A _____ like<u>s</u> to sneak <u>into</u>
   the cave.
   snore   snake   smile

4. The _____ make<u>s</u> me slide on the
   road.
   sleet   snore   slice

5. A _____ of cake would be nice
   to eat.
   slide   slice   slave

6. You can make a _____ on the
   face.
              slime   smile   slide

Book I Bg.   Lesson 50 ee=y   Integral 87

Teacher: Student makes some p+j words into two beat (syllable) words by add-
ing ee to the word he prints in the second column. Because we do not let ee
hang out at the end of a syllabled word (most of the time), the student must
now make y act like a hook to pull the ee out. (He marks over the ee.) Be
sure he understands why he is doing this procedure. (Reteach Lessons 28 and 32.)
Student then copies the word in its final form in the last column. Take the
student through the first word or two as he tells you what he has to do.

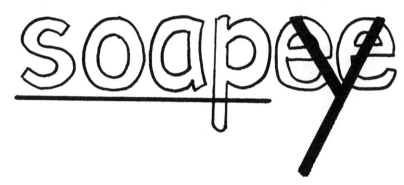

soap	soapee	soapy
foam		
beef		
hair		
teak		
need		
rain		
leaf		
weep		
meat		

Book I Bg.   Lesson 50 ee=y   Integral 87

Teacher: In order to make layer cake words into the two beat words with <u>ee</u>
last sound, the student has to complete an extra step. First he scrapes off
<u>e</u> frosting by printing the word without the <u>e</u>. Second he adds the <u>ee</u> letter
to represent the long <u>e</u> sound and then puts the <u>y</u> hook over the <u>ee</u>. Third
he copies the word in its final form.

haze   haze   hazee   hazy

	1st	2nd	3rd
haze	haz	hazee	hazy
cage			
face			
rose			
wave			
bone			
tide			
dope			
nose			

Book I Bg.   Lesson 51 <u>sc</u> <u>sk</u> <u>sp</u>   Integrals 88-90

1. Would you eat slimy meat? _____

2. Can you skate on the ice? _____

3. Is a spike like a huge nail? _____

4. Would a m<u>on</u>ster with slimy f<u>eet and a</u>
   greasy, grimy face scare you? _____

5. Did you see the score of the game? _____

1. Is the sky green? _____

2. Would you speak to a m<u>on</u>ster? _____

3. Do you feel you <u>can have</u> a speedy
   drive in a jeep? _____

4. <u>Could</u> you keep the score in the game?
   _____

5. Can Craig skate in the sky? _____

Book I Bg.   Lesson 51 Capital O   Integral 91

Teacher: Student traces o's in the picture starting at the stars. He then
prints lower case o's on the first line below the picture, capital O's on
the second line, and sets of capital O followed by lower case o on the third
line. Be sure he starts at the correct point and moves to say, "Hi, hand"
("Bye, hand" for lefty).

Book I Bg.   Lesson 51 <u>-ed</u>   Integral 92

Teacher: Students are to add <u>-ed</u> suffix to those words that they can
change into yesterday time. Remind them these will be action words.
There will be some students in a class that can go through these pages
very quickly and need more challenge. They can use the WORD LISTS in
their storybooks to add more words to the activity. They also can
make up sentences using the words. The student with problems may only
be able to tolerate a small portion of the sheet. Let each student
succeed by assigning what he or she can manage.

pray	drain	heal
week	grain	blade
toad	stay	drake
smear	hair	rain
meal	coal	clear
greet	dream	dear
play	need	fear
groan	braid	leak

Book I Bg.   Lesson 52 <u>st</u>   Integral 93

1. Would you like to eat paste? _____

2. Can a seal race up the stair<u>s</u>? _____

3. Would a deer sleep in the stove? _____

4. Can you buy a roast in the store? _____

5. Is it fine to waste heat? _____

1. Is going to the store a treat for you?
   _____

2. Would a goat like to swing on a tree?
   _____

3. Do you like roast beef? _____

4. Could Jake baste the meat ?
   _____

5. Do you have a stain on your sleeve?
   _____

Book I Bg.   Lesson 52 <u>st</u>   Integral 93

Teacher: Student colors as follows:

<u>st</u> + p+j____red
<u>st</u> + l-c____blue

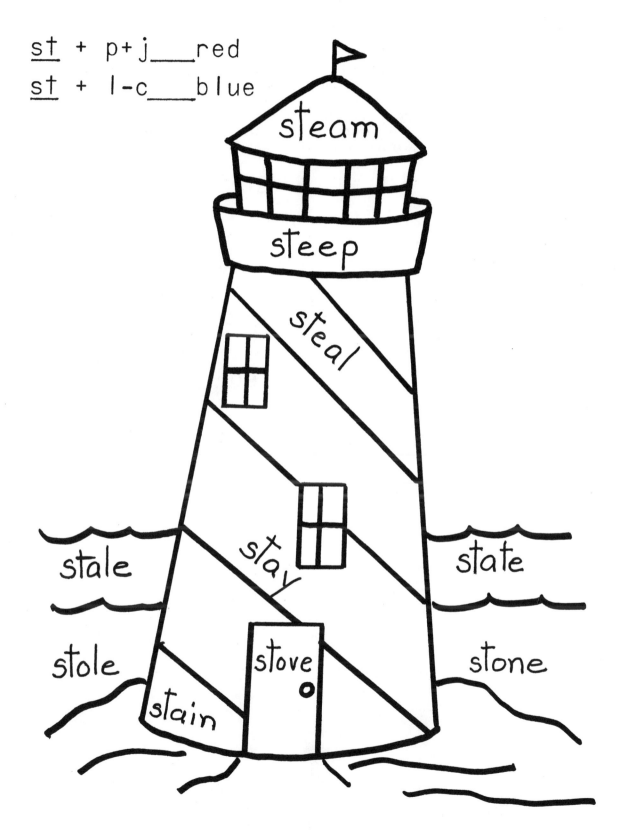

Teacher: Read the teacher's instructions carefully in your manual before you
explain this page to your class. You will need to take your students individu-
ally or in no more than three in a group through this activity. State that
the first column of <u>sai</u> represents the way we would like to spell <u>say</u>. In the
second column the student is to scratch out the diagonal <u>y</u> line and dot the other
line to make it look like a tipsy <u>i</u>. Then he prints <u>sai</u> in the third column.
Next he crosses out the <u>e</u> of <u>ed</u>. Now he has the finished word <u>said</u> which should
be pronounced with a long <u>a</u> but is not. He does the same procedure with <u>pay</u>.
We have <u>pay</u> as now time and <u>paid</u> as yesterday time. It would be wise to copy
this page for the student to do several times. These instructions are complex.
Be very patient. You are training more skills than appears on the surface.

sai   say = sai   ed   said

sai   say = _____   ed _____

sai   say = _____   ed _____

sai   say = _____   ed _____

pai   pay = _____   ed _____

pai   pay = _____   ed _____

pai   pay = _____   ed _____

1. Can a train eat toast? _____

2. Could you slide on a tray on a slope?
_____

3. Can Craig drive a jeep on a trail? _____

4. Can you sweep your home? _____

5. Would Grace like to sleep in a tree
home? _____

1. Would a tree sway in the breeze? _____

2. Would you eat sweet toast? _____

3. Would grease be a treat to eat? _____

4. Would you trade a bike for a nail? _____

5. Can Jake train a seal? _____

Book I Bg.   Lesson 53 <u>tr</u> <u>sw</u>   Integrals 95, 96

Teacher: Student reads the words to find which ones he can add <u>ed</u> to. He
prints them below with the <u>ed</u> ending. Be sure to review the fact that he
has to scrape off the <u>e</u> frosting.

sway	train	trace
sweet	tray	swore
treat	trail	trade

<u>ed</u>

Book I Bg.   Lesson 53 Capitals <u>K</u> <u>Z</u> <u>U</u>   Integrals 97-99

Teacher: Student prints several times the capital first and then the lower case form of each of the letters. Be sure he starts at the correct point. He may decorate the page as he wishes.

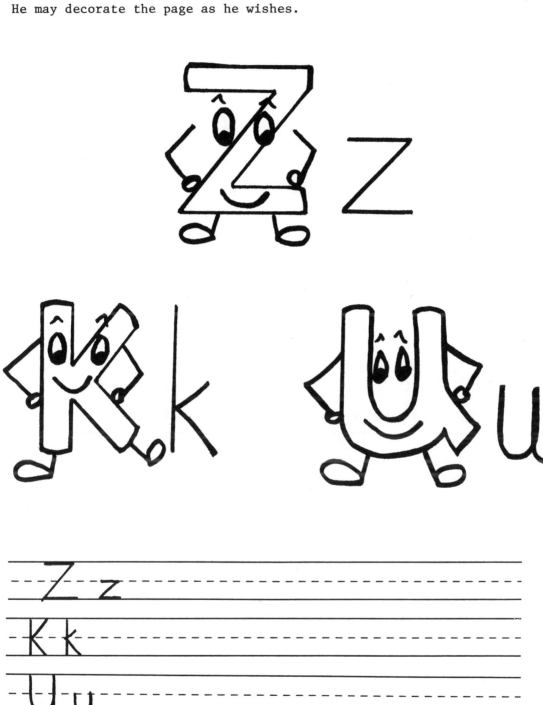

Teacher: You can cut out one of these sections for each of five days. See
directions in Lesson 9.

1. Make a green stripe on a boat.
2. Make Craig scream. 3. Make a strike
in a game. 4. Make Jake scrape a plate.

1. Make spray from a boat. 2. Make a
plate of toast. 3. Make a train.
4. Make Dean sweep.

1. Make a trail. 2. Make a stream by the
road. 3. Make a stove. 4. Make a stain
on a coat.

1. Make sleet. 2. Make Jean skate on the
ice. 3. Make an ice cream cone. 4. Make
a spear.

1. Make a streak of grease on his feet.
2. Make Jane steal a base. 3. Make smoke
in a fire. 4. Make Grace snore.

Book I Bg.   Lesson 54 <u>str</u> <u>scr</u> <u>spr</u>   Integrals 100-102

Teacher: Student finds and circles the words in the puzzle – across and up
to down only. He may cross off the line beside the word in the column after
he finds the word in the puzzle. He writes the words in the spaces below.
He can decorate the page afterwards.

scrape |

scream |

screen |

sprain |

strain |

streak |

stripe |

stroke |

```
s  p  r  a  i  n  n  s  c
t  s  c  r  e  a  m  c  e
r  c  e  h  n  m  u  r  n
a  r  n  s  t  r  e  a  k
i  e  c  o  l  h  n  p  g
n  e  s  t  r  i  p  e  p
u  n  m  s  t  r  o  k  e
```

Book I Bg.   Lesson 54 <u>str</u> <u>scr</u>

Teacher: Student colors as follows:

Integrals 100, 101

<u>str</u> + p+j____green
<u>str</u> + l-c____red
<u>sc</u> + p+j____blue
<u>sc</u> + l-c____yellow
<u>scr</u> + p+j____brown
<u>sk</u> + l-c____orange
<u>sw</u> + p+j____purple

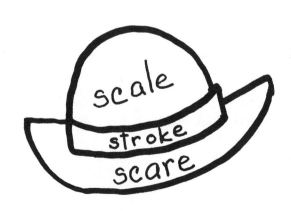